Norman, 1938 - 1971

Anthony Astbury

Mailer Press, London

First published in this edition in 2008 by Mailer Press,
50 Comeragh Road, London W14 9HR

mailerpress@googlemail.com
www.mailerpress.co.uk

ISBN   978 0 9560286 0 0

Printed in Great Britain

In memory of Mrs. Mary Chadwick

His death has stunned me into something like Belief.

Our last talk in the 'Zetland' – Poetry – 'I want to know about this guy' – after I had quoted Wallace Steven's line 'And there I found myself more truly and more strange' from 'The Emperor of Ice-Cream' which excited us both so much.

In my address book I have just put Mrs. Chadwick's name over Norman's crossed-out one. I shall send her a Christmas card forever.

The funeral service – so many *there* – packed – 'We did him proud.'

Re the church and its efficacy – it has to be admitted that we *all* needed the ritual of the funeral service.

Brian talking so movingly about Norman and quoting Dylan's 'After the first death there is no other.'

See you in Heaven, Norman.

I still haven't wept – that's what bothers me.

Irrevocably depleted.

He is my first death.

Norman beat us all to it – showed us the final way too.

The worst thing that's happened to me for years.

How brave and noble Mrs. Chadwick was......

I am going to write a poem/elegy worthy of him.

He was a great man.

I kept getting the date wrong – I didn't know what day it was.

Norman must have walked every inch of Bury.

His death – disappearance has put the whole of Life into meaningful context for me.

The funeral service was every bit as bad as I had feared.

We are always sad when a genius dies. Norman had a genius for people.

Why I didn't go across to Lytham to see my parents or stay on with Brian – I wanted out – to leave Lancashire and be alone with my grief in the hope that a poem would come.

Telegram to Brian – heart-broken.

As always, I plunge into books to get over a bad patch in my life.

If ever I have been guilty of taking anyone I liked and who liked me for granted I've learned the truth now.

I haven't been as *set-back* for years.

I'll never forget: my coffin handle (plastic) snapped off as I helped to carry him to the final place.

Due to Norman – for the first time *ever* the thought occurred to me to go back to live in *our* town – Bury.

The horror of the manner of his death.

I'm so glad he came to see me in Warwick just before the end.

A whole generation in Bury won't get over this, pubs and clubs be the same again.

I have just crossed out Norman's name in my address book.

I feel incapable of writing to his mother.

Only Love and exorcise Death.

Deeply ironic that because Norman was at last 'making it' – money (he was on the brink of buying his long dreamed of 'perfect scene' up in the hills) – the big car – killed him.

Leo thought that Norman – dear, wild, spontaneous Norman hadn't been able to resist a 'burn-up' on the quiet country road – the hole in the surface waiting…….

As I said to Kath in 'our' pub, the Tubs after the service – in the face of such ultimate happenings – for the first time truly experienced – only confirmed/crystallized what has long been taking shape, namely there is only one answer/feeling to death – God – Faith – the extra dimension outside and yet transcending the human. I believe it's all we've got.

Someone who truly loved me has died.

I recollect my conversation with Peter before the dear death – about Rodin, Rilke, Pasternak, Schoenberg, Stravinsky, Dylan Thomas – and their belief in someone/something – some First Cause as Powys put it. If such men as these believe in something beyond man who am I to argue? But, as always, one has to find out the hard way – for oneself alone – only then can one truly feel that kind of faith – just as in Life only by living fearlessly can one come to love and trust.

Norman's death has helped me grow up.

Our last conversation: The Grandeur of Bachelors!

Norman and I were closest when we first met – despite
everything since – and played as teen-agers for Bolton Rd.
Methodists football team – wing half me stroking it
through to the courageous, slogging inside forward.
That's how I'll always remember him – supreme *trier*.

1971

For Norman Chadwick (1938 – 1971)

Nothing that I could write now or then would do you

Justice Norman – even suggest your greatness – just as in

Life nothing I could say or do would appease

Your look – and now nothing I am excludes you.

1974